# Contents

# Kokomo Blues

Standard Tuning

Scrapper Blackwell

Damp Bass Throughout...

**Alt. Verse**

6

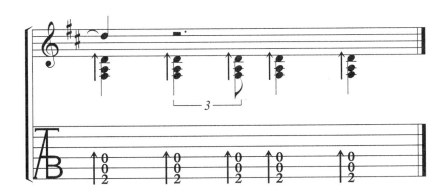

# Blue Day Blues

Standard Tuning

Scrapper Blackwell

Damp bass...

simile throughout...

8

To BREAK...

9

**Break**

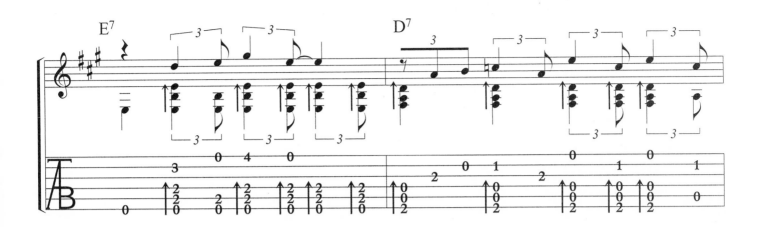

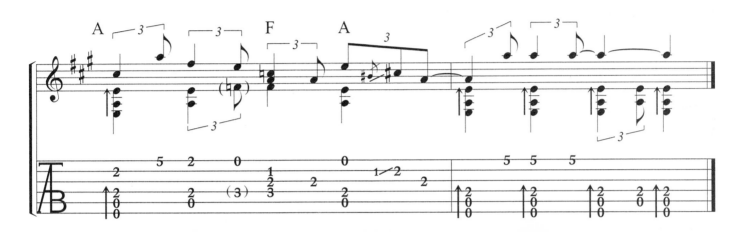

Scrapper Blackwell

# Devil Got My Woman

Cross-Note Tuning—D minor: DADFAD

### Intro & 1st Verse

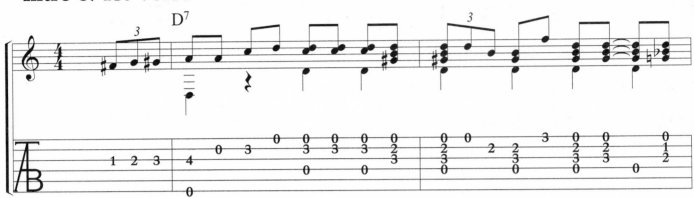

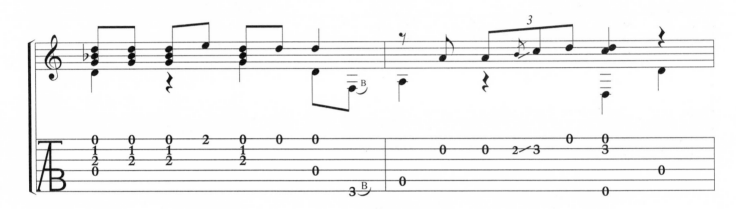

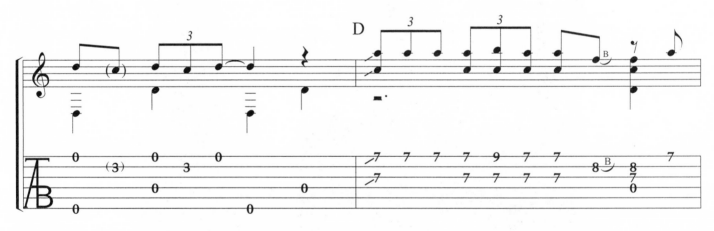

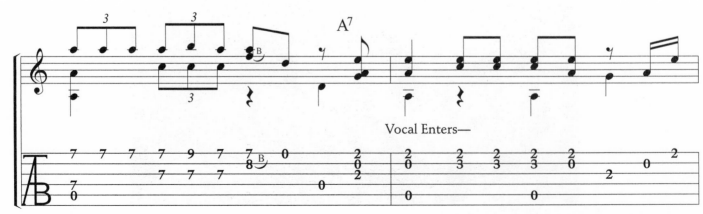

Vocal Enters—

To Next Verse…

# My Black Mama

Spanish Tuning: DGDGBD

Son House

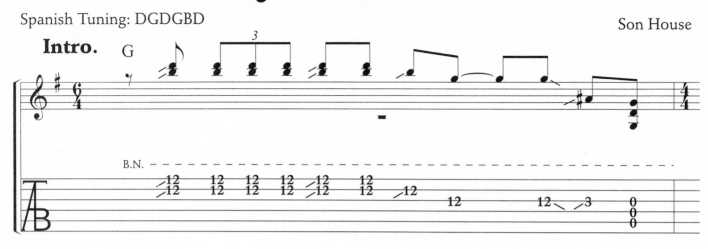

**Verse**

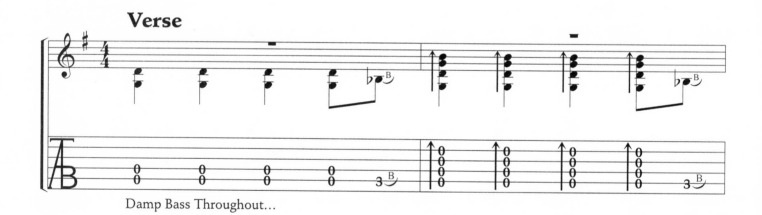

Damp Bass Throughout...

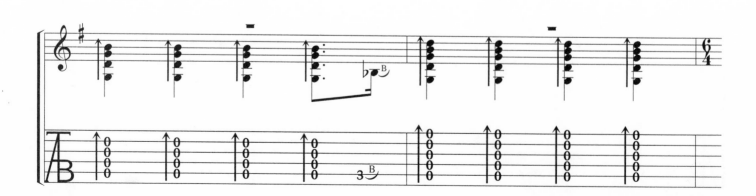

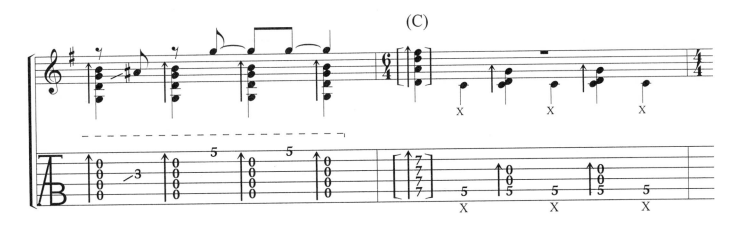

(C)

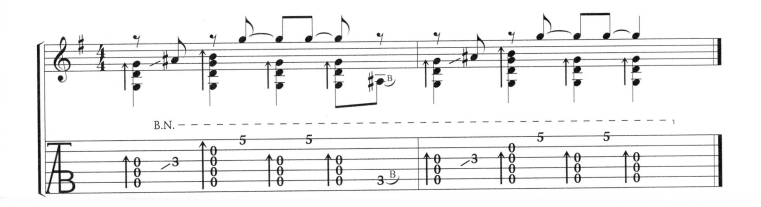

15

# Roll and Tumble Blues

Spanish Tuning: DGDGBD

Willie Newbern

Bottleneck Throughout...

16

## Alternate 1st Four Bars

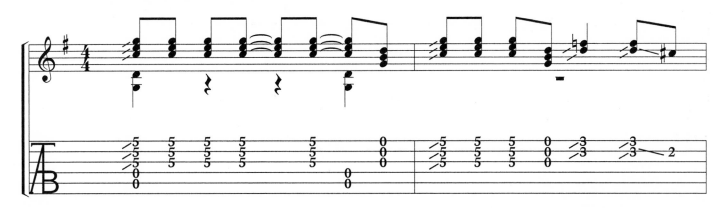

# Screamin' and Hollerin' the Blues

Spanish Tuning: DGDGBD

Charlie Patton

### Intro. (Pick-Up)

(X = Hit Guitar and String)

### Verse 1

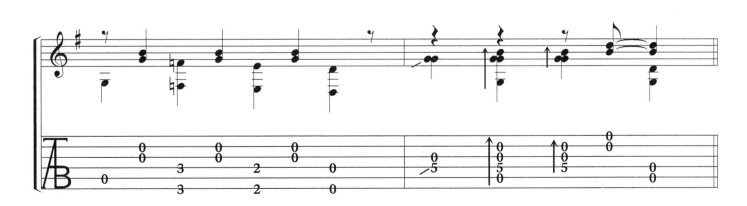

## Alternate Verse

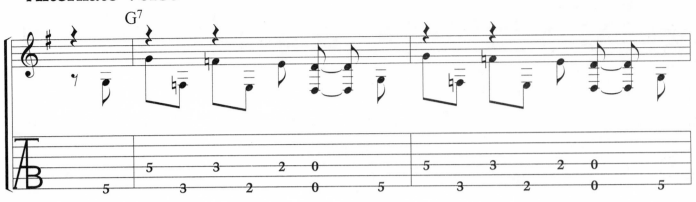

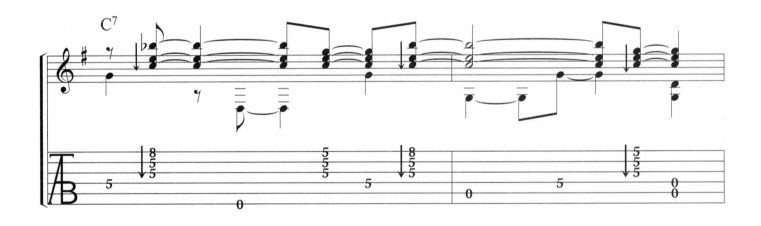

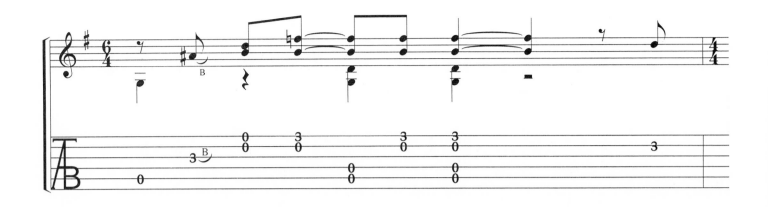

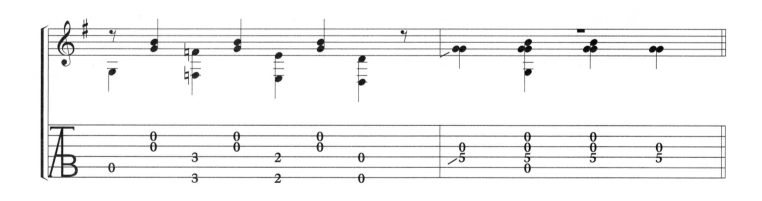

## 1st Variation — 1st Four Bars

## 2nd Variation — 1st Four Bars

# Life Saver Blues

Tuning: DADGBE

Lonnie Johnson

**Verse**

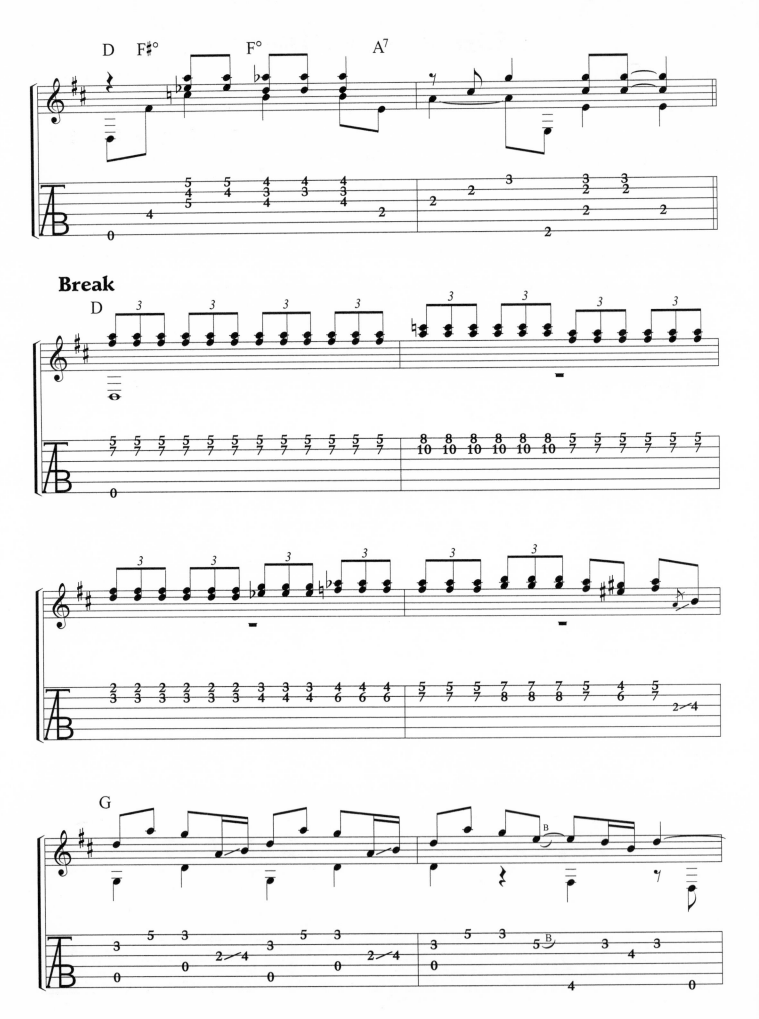

**Break**

24

# Georgia Bound

Standard Tuning

*Fast* **Intro.**

Blind Blake

To Verse…

**Verse 1**

26

## Break 1

28

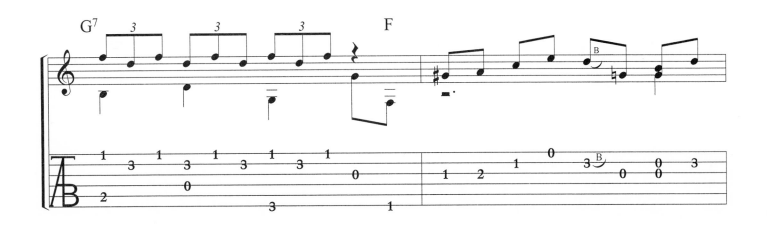

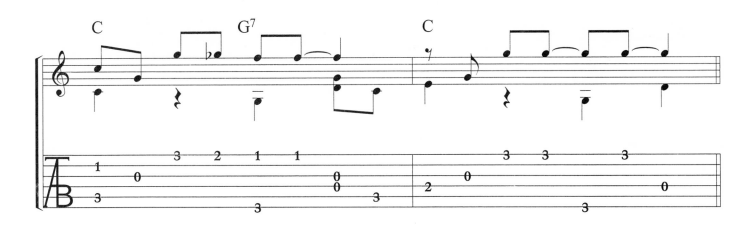

**Break 2**

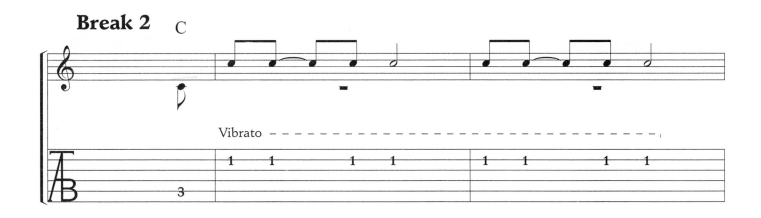

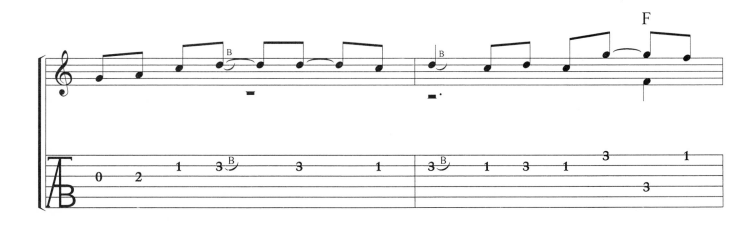

Blind Blake

Son House